WALT DISNEY

A Life From Beginning to End

Copyright © 2018 by Hourly History.

All rights reserved.

Table of Contents

Introduction
Humble Beginnings
Hard Work and All Play
Serving in World War I
Disney, Iwerks, and Innovation
Methods and Matrimony
The Lucky Rabbit and Mickey Mouse
The Road to Success
Impeccable Timing
From Snow White to Pinocchio
Disney During World War II
Going to Disneyland
Conclusion

Introduction

The name Disney is celebrated all throughout the world because of its association with blockbuster animated films and most especially iconic cartoon characters. Just about everyone on the planet, regardless of time, place, or culture, has at one time or another become acquainted with Mickey Mouse, Donald Duck, and everybody's favorite anthropomorphic dog, Goofy. These are the characters that we all know and love.

And in recent years Disney has become set to become even larger—an entire galaxy in fact—by adopting a new host of characters from George Lucas' Star Wars franchise. It seems that the name Disney, even 50 some years after Walt Disney's death, is destined to get even bigger. But as much as we can associate the name Disney with all of these incredible feature films, it is amazing how little most people know about Walt Disney himself.

Few know of Disney's humble upbringing in rural America, learning to draw farm animals and flowers. Very few know the origin of Mickey Mouse, and even fewer know of the role that Donald Duck played during the war effort of World War II. Walt Disney led a life that was just as epic as the stories he helped to bring about. Come along as we present to you a tale just as fascinating as any plot sequence to have ever graced Walt Disney's storyboard.

Chapter One

Humble Beginnings

"The way to get started is to quit talking and begin doing."

—Walt Disney

Born into a modest Chicago home on December 5, 1901, Walt came from a long line of Disneys. His ancestry was said to hail back to a man named Jean Christophe D'Isigny who had hitched a ride with William the Conqueror in 1066 as he laid siege to England. You see, the Disneys were originally from somewhere off the shores of Normandy, France before they made their way to England, and as was customary of the time, they anglicized their name by changing it from D'Isigny to Disney.

Although the Disneys may have arrived in England as conquerors, several centuries later they were mostly simple farmers in Britain's Ireland. Instead of raising cane, they were most likely raising other more peaceful crops. It was in 1834, a decade before the great Irish potato famine, that a branch of the Disney family decided to try their luck in the New World of America. By the time of Walt Disney's birth in 1901, many of the Disney family members had spread far and wide in the United States, engaging in many different modes of living and occupations.

When Walt Disney was born, his father Elias was employed as a carpenter and was working for a local pastor on a church construction project. That pastor's name was Walter Parr, and Elias was apparently so taken with the minister he decided to name his son after him, bequeathing him with the official name of Walter Elias Disney or as he would become better known, Walt Disney.

Chapter Two

Hard Work and All Play

"If you can dream it, you can do it."

—Walt Disney

Due to an increasing disaffection for city life and also in part to his father's rampant gambling debts at Chicago saloons, the Disney family picked up and left the Windy City in 1903. Their next destination would be several hundred miles further west in Marceline, Missouri—far enough away for Elias to get a new start and for the debt collectors not to follow. The first job that Walt Disney's father fell into was working as a laborer on his brother Robert's apple farm.

Apparently eschewing his life as a roving gambler for good, Elias worked hard in his brother's apple orchards until he had enough money to purchase 40 acres of his own land, just a few years after his arrival, in 1906. Elias then began growing apples on his land and put his two oldest sons Raymond and Herbert to work with him on their family farm. In 1909, however, 21-year-old Raymond and 20-year-old Herbert grew weary of life on the farm and left to seek their fortunes elsewhere.

Their departure left a much greater burden on Elias and his two remaining sons, 16-year-old Roy and 8-year-old Walt. Unfortunately for them, it seems that their father began to take out his growing frustration on his younger sons as a result. It is said that Elias soon became an even stricter authoritarian than he already was and always ready to take a belt to Roy and Walt's backside if he felt they needed his correction. Under such stringent conditions, Walt's relationship with his father seemed to have been understandably strained.

It was to his mother Flora that Walt most often looked to for comfort growing up, and it was also from her that he was first introduced to the world of imagination that would become the hallmark of his career. Disney's mother would read to him bedtime stories sparking the child's early creativity with fairy tales and folkloric legends that would stick with him for the rest of his life.

Walt's time on the apple farm would come to a close in 1909 when his father contracted pneumonia and the family farm's profits dropped low enough to prompt him to sell it. It was then that Elias Disney—constantly on the search for the next opportunity—picked up his family once again and moved them to Kansas City, Missouri so that he could try his hand at a large newspaper delivery route that he had just purchased.

Today, it may seem odd for a grown man to sell a farm to deliver newspapers, but back in 1909, before TV and when radio was still in its infancy, the vast majority of Americans still read and subscribed to newspapers. Newspaper delivery was a big and profitable business, with eager investors buying larger shares of delivery routes all the time. The franchise that Elias Disney purchased in Kansas City was no exception, and by all accounts, he expected to get a big return on his investment.

Like always, he also expected his sons to take part in helping him earn those profits. The Disney brothers Roy and Walt could be seen out every day of the week delivering newspapers. This entailed young Walt having to wake up just before four in the morning to make his rounds. This soon took quite a toll on the young Disney who had to attend elementary school as well as his morning paper delivery.

It is said that he was often so exhausted that he would sneak quick naps during those early morning hours in the alleyways just outside the homes of the customers, in between deliveries. Things then got even more difficult for Walt, when in 1911, shortly after turning 18, his older brother Roy decided to move out of his parents' house, and strike it on his own. Walt was around ten years old at the time and now had the unenviable task of having to take over all the work that his big brother had left behind. Despite these rigors, however, the young Walt Disney struggled on and even managed to find a new calling for himself.

It was in his school's art class that he began to find the outlet for expression that he had so long sought. On one particular occasion that his teachers would later remember, the class was sat before a collection of flowers and instructed to draw them as realistically as possible. This was an endeavor that young Walt seemed to relish and he completely threw himself into the task at hand. But as one of the instructors peered over Disney's shoulder to see what he was drawing, he was amazed to find that Walt not only drew the flowers as he saw them; he drew them as his imagination saw them, drawing human-like faces on each of the flowers and hands growing out of their stems.

Disney, of course, would later become famous for his cartoonish portrayals and anthropomorphizing of inanimate objects, but to his teachers at the time, it struck them as odd. In the early 1900s such things were not too common, and they didn't have much of a reference point to appreciate cartoonish, smiling flowers. It had never been done before. But as they say, there is a first time for everything, and one day the whole world would come to appreciate the vision Walt Disney wished to convey to them.

Chapter Three

Serving in World War I

"The more you like yourself, the less you are like anyone else, which makes you unique."

—Walt Disney

By 1917 the Disney household was facing major changes once again when Walt's father decided to sell the newspaper route business for $16,000 and move the family back to Chicago. Elias had his sights on—of all things—a jelly factory, and used his proceeds from the paper route to purchase the facility.

Walt Disney was now around 15 years old and enrolled to attend Chicago's McKinley High School. It was here that he was given his first official mode of expression when he was given a position to draw cartoons in the school newspaper. As hostilities heated up in Europe in the war that would become known as World War I, Walt found a regular role for himself in penning cartoonish skits of military personnel fighting the war.

Young and impressionable Walt had no idea of just how dreadful it was in the trenches of Europe, and his fanciful renderings lacked any firsthand knowledge of what the war to end all wars was really all about. But shortly after America entered the conflict, joining the

British and French Allies to fight against the Germans on April 6, 1917, Disney sought to join up himself. His brother Roy, now 24 years old, had already been recruited, and Walt ever eager to follow in his brother's footsteps wished to enlist as well. He wasn't old enough, however, and would need his parents' permission.

Walt's parents were understandably hesitant to send their young son to a war zone. Not wishing to argue the finer points of patriotism with his parents any further, Walt decided to take matters into his own hands and forged his parents' signatures. He was then selected to train with the Red Cross ambulance corps in the fall of 1918, but by the time Disney arrived in Europe later that November, the armistice that ended World War I had already been signed and the fighting had ceased. To Walt's disappointment—and his worried mother Flora's immense relief—he would not see any action in the European theatre of war.

Nevertheless, Walt received plenty of work in southern France tending to the many injured veterans of World War I. And when he wasn't tending to the wounded vets, young Walt was being introduced to some less altruistic activities. For the first time completely away from the strict oversight of his parents, Disney began to indulge himself in a bit of carousing.

This exploration of his newfound freedoms culminated in a raucous 18th birthday party that his co-workers in the ambulance corps threw for him. For this milestone, Disney is said to have drank hard liquor, smoked, and enjoyed the attention of a pretty young woman from that evening and on into the small hours of the morning. But besides engaging in mischief such as this, as more and more of his potential patients were shipped home, there really wasn't that much else for Walt Disney to do.

As a result, Disney quickly found himself bored enough to delve back into his old pastime of artwork by painting the sides of ambulances with improvised cartoonish depictions of his co-workers. These imaginative murals on the sides of the vehicles apparently impressed one of the soldiers in attendance, and he recruited Walt to join him on a money-making scheme of his.

The soldier apparently wanted to take captured German surplus helmets that were just laying around and mock them up to look like used equipment pulled directly from the battlefield. To do this Walt and the soldier had the previously pristine and unused helmets taken and used for target practice and riddled with bullets. The now quite worn and torn gear was then handed over to Walt who used the best of his artistic ability to paint German wartime decorations on the helmets. The two would then sell the battered helmets as war trophies, and after it was all said and done Walt made about 300 dollars from the enterprise.

At the end of his tour of duty, Walt Disney took a steamship back to the United States. After landing in New York, he left by train for Chicago where he spent some time with his parents. He didn't stay long and was soon on another train heading to Kansas City where he sought to move in with his older brother Roy and start his career as a cartoonist in earnest.

Disney spent the next few days looking for work, and when he couldn't immediately find it, he became terribly depressed. His brother Roy, ever his saving grace in life, was able to pull him out of the dumps. He was soon able to get an interview lined up for Walt with the local Pressman-Rubin Commercial Art Studio for a job as a commercial artist. Walt was beside himself with joy; he felt that he had at last been given his opportunity. Eager to make a good impression, he brought his whole portfolio in for his debut, and to his immense delight, he managed to get the job.

Chapter Four

Disney, Iwerks, and Innovation

"I believe in being an innovator."

—Walt Disney

Walt Disney was excited to finally work for a real art studio and worked with passion and due diligence on whatever was assigned to him. Most of his assignments consisted of drawing cartoons advertising farm equipment such as tractors and silo lifts. Unfortunately for Disney, however, as passionate as he was for his work, after his first review he was laid off for what Pressman-Rubin Studios referred to as a "singular lack of drawing ability"—a stinging rebuke for someone who was trying to make their living as a sketch artist.

With no other means of income Walt had no choice but to temporarily shelve his dreams of being an artist. He got a job at the post office instead; depression would follow shortly after that. During much of the Christmas season of 1919, he would trudge home from his postal job and go directly to his room, avoiding all company and conversation.

But then just days before the coming New Year, Walt received a surprise visitor. It was a man named Ub Iwerks whom Walt had worked with at the studio. As it turned out, he had been laid off from his job as a commercial artist as well. The young men, becoming bolstered by their common experience and growing solidarity, proceeded to talk late into the night about their future plans and possibilities.

During their conversation, they came up with the idea of starting their own company. They felt that if no one wanted to hire them, then they should hire themselves in their very own art studio. It was from this brainstorming session that the two conceptualized what they would call Iwerks-Disney Commercial Artists. They were both essentially freelance artists now, and over the next few days Walt took it upon himself to call around town, securing minor assignments here and there to stay afloat. But it wasn't nearly enough to get by, and both Disney and Iwerks soon realized they needed to seek work elsewhere.

Walt Disney's opening to escape the moribund partnership came in late January 1920 when he was hired by Kansas City Film Ad Company as a commercial artist, making $40 a week. This wasn't a bad paycheck at all in 1920, and it was certainly much more than the already defunct Iwerks-Disney partnership could have provided, so Walt jumped at the opportunity.

Iwerks followed shortly thereafter, also getting hired on at Kansas City Film Ad Company, reviving the partnership at least unofficially, under the Film Ad

Company's auspices. Here Disney and Iwerks employed a crude form of animation that utilized cut out drawings moved in front of the camera on handheld wooden posts that they were affixed to. As humble as it may have been, this was Walt Disney's first foray into work as an animator.

He was intrigued by the practice and sought to perfect his ability with it by practicing during his downtime with his own drawings in front of the camera. It was during this experimentation that Disney concluded that frame-by-frame animation would be best. Disney tried to broach his findings with his superiors at Kansas City Film Ad Company, but they wouldn't have it. This rejection of his findings and recommendation prompted Disney to once again start his own company, which he called Laugh-O-Grams.

With his animation production company established, Disney took some of the work he had created in his free time and introduced them to Frank Newman, the manager of a string of movie theatres in the greater Kansas City area. Newman was impressed enough to begin showing Disney's short animation skits in between films. With his initial success with Newman's theatres, Disney decided to resign from his position with the Kansas City Film Ad Company to cast his lots with Newman fulltime.

In May 1921, Disney set up his own studio, naming it Laugh-O-Gram Studio. Iwerks would join Disney in this endeavor as well and immediately began work on a version of *Alice in Wonderland*, which involved an actress playing the role of Alice superimposed on an animated background. Before production was finished, Disney, always looking ahead, contacted Margaret Winkler in New York, who was a big-time distributor of animated shorts.

Winkler was already famous for her stewardship of the classic Felix the Cat cartoon and was looking for the next big thing. She was intrigued by Disney's idea of combining live action over a cartoon backdrop and, thinking that his kind of improvisation just might be what she was looking for, she encouraged him to finish his efforts so that she could see the final product.

Disney was now giddy with enthusiasm and put himself and his partner Iwerks into an extremely tight deadline to get everything finished on time. They worked around the clock to get the project completed, but it proved to be much more time consuming than Disney had thought, and they wouldn't be able to make the deadline after all.

Meanwhile, with all of their effort placed in the *Alice in Wonderland* project, their bills and expenses were mounting. Unable to continue and unsure of where else to go, Disney disbanded Laugh-O-Gram Studio in July 1923, bought a ticket for California, and paid a visit to his brother, Roy. He hoped that the change of venue would bring him a change in fortune.

Just like his father before him, who had skipped town in Chicago in order to escape his rampant gambling debts, Disney too hoped to give his creditors and naysayers the slip. He wished to take his vision elsewhere and start anew amidst the glitz and glamour of Hollywood, California.

Chapter Five

Methods and Matrimony

"When you're curious, you find lots of interesting things to do."

—Walt Disney

Shortly after his arrival in California, Disney restabilized his contacts with the famed animation maven of the East Coast, Margaret Winkler. Disney sent Winkler a letter explaining his current plight and future ambition in the industry. It seems that Disney reached out to her at just the right time. She was in the process of losing artistic control over her previous headline act, Felix the Cat, and was actively seeking a new one.

Upon receiving Disney's message, Winkler lent a sympathetic ear to the young entrepreneur and expressed her faith in his vision. But she also stressed that he needed to raise money for an advertising campaign if he ever wished to get any traction for his work. And so, after borrowing $785 from family members to get the ball rolling, Walt Disney, just 22 years of age, entered into an official contract with Margaret Winkler on October 16, 1923.

The deal entailed the production of a total of at least six of Disney's *Alice in Wonderland* episodes. Eager to get started on production, Walt and his brother Roy rented some office space for $10 and began work. Walt quickly finished up a series of shorts entitled *Alice Hunting in Africa* and sent it off to Winkler in New York. Upon her review of the material, Margaret still expressed interest and encouraged Disney to proceed, but she stressed that she felt that there was a decided lack of humor in the final production.

For a series of cartoon skits that were meant by nature to be humorous, it must have struck Disney as a stinging reprimand to be told that his work wasn't funny enough. Nevertheless, he rapidly fired off another finished production called *Alice's Spooky Adventures*, which depicted the main character and her various hijinks in a ghost and goblin-filled landscape. With this switch of plot and characterization, Disney apparently hit the mark, and Winkler readily approved the distribution of the work.

Disney's production made its debut in March 1924 at several movie theatres all along the Eastern Seaboard. Disney was in for a disappointment that August, however, when poor box office returns for his Alice series prompted Winkler to reduce his advance payouts from $1,500 to $900. This was a depressing blow to Disney, and the fact that audiences weren't receptive to his work was more painful to him than the monetary cutback.

Shortly after this development, Winkler married a one-time booking agent for Warner Brothers named Charles B. Mintz. And, in a move that was quite telling of the times they were living in, the newlywed Margaret Mintz immediately relinquished all of the authority of her distribution company over to her husband. Now all future negotiations for Disney's contract would go directly through Charles B. Mintz.

Upon hearing this news, Disney in turn handed over the deal-making end of the company to his brother, Roy. It was not a decision that Walt would regret. After Mintz and Roy began a dialogue with each other, Roy managed to cut a deal even better than what they had before. He was able to convince Mintz to pay out $1,800 per Alice episode for a total of 18 short films. Roy's skill as a negotiator would become a hallmark of the Disney brothers' partnership.

Disney was the creative force and his brother Roy was the deal maker. But despite their cozy relationship as business partners, the many long hours spent together would soon bring some deterioration to their personal relationship. Walt seemed to revel in the bachelor life they shared, enjoying nothing more than working in the studio then coming home to his brother to hammer out the finer details of the next day's work, late into the night.

Roy, however, began to detest their home life together and sought a way out. He found it by reconnecting with a girlfriend from Kansas City named Edna Francis. Walt at first seemed resentful of the relationship and was even said to consider it a kind of interference and betrayal of their professional partnership. Nevertheless, Roy would go on to marry Edna on April 7, 1925.

Walt, ever the competitor with his brother, decided to follow suit. Soon after his brother's marriage to Edna, he began dating Lillian Bounds, who was one of the bridesmaids at Roy and Edna's wedding. In incredibly fast fashion, Walt Disney then took Lillian to be his wife just a few months on the heels of his brother's wedding, marrying Lillian Bounds on July 25, 1925.

The two newest of the Disney newlyweds departed for what could only be called a working honeymoon with Walt's mind often being elsewhere. He even cut the outing short, insisting they had to return early due to pressing matters at his studio that needed his attention. But even though his mind often wandered, just like the fairy tales he so relished in his childhood, the bond he forged with Lillian would prove permanent. He would remain married to her for the rest of his life.

Chapter Six

The Lucky Rabbit and Mickey Mouse

"I only hope that we don't lose sight of one thing—that it was all started by a mouse."

—Walt Disney

In 1926, Walt Disney had just finished construction on a new studio when Charles Mintz arrived to deliver some devastating news—he was ending Disney's contract. Disney was not prepared to receive such a dire directive, and he is said to have completely isolated himself, barely coming out of his office over the next few days.

What Disney didn't know was that Mintz had been in the process of talks with the founder of Universal Studios, Carl Laemmle. Mintz and Laemmle had been discussing the prospects of creating a character that could compete with the still dominating Felix the Cat cartoon. As a result of their brainstorming they came up with the idea of an animated bunny rabbit. Now all they needed was an animator.

It was in this fashion that Mintz arrived at the door of Disney's studio once again with an offer to have Disney bring life to their conceptualized rabbit. Mintz informed

Disney that the contract could indeed be salvaged if his team could come up with a good take on the character. Not wanting to lose his contract, Disney and his team jumped at the chance and worked feverishly to make Mintz's vision come to life. The result of their efforts was Oswald the Lucky Rabbit.

After approval, Disney's work then culminated in the 1927 release of the short film called *Trolley Troubles*. This debut was well received, and Oswald the Lucky Rabbit seemed poised to become a fan favorite. Believing this success would take him to newfound prosperity, in February 1928 near the end of his contract Walt sought to negotiate a better deal for himself. But in a move that would leave Disney once again devastated, instead of agreeing to pay him more for his work, Mintz insisted that Disney take a pay cut instead.

Mintz informed the cartoonist that his payments for finished productions would be cut from $2,250 down to $1,800 per release. Mintz then gave Disney the sobering reminder that he controlled all the rights to the character that Disney had created. Even though Disney's team that put down the ink for Oswald, it was Mintz and Laemmle that owned the bunny rabbit's soul. He furthermore reminded Disney that he would hire most of his staff to continue projection of Oswald "with or without" Disney's input.

Disney didn't directly respond to these threats and ultimatums and is said to have excused himself and walked out of Mintz's office without saying another word. By the time Disney got back to his studio, he discovered that Mintz had already made good on his promise of recruiting the Disney staff. Walt found that over half of his employees had turned in their resignations and switched over to Mintz's team.

Mintz, figuring Disney had no choice but to accept his terms, again offered him a deal, but Disney could only tell him that he would think about it. Walt then conferred with his brother Roy about the ordeal, and Roy urged him to accept Mintz's new contract, advising him that they could take the cut, save the studio, and simply come up with a new character that would be all their own. Disney then made his way back to Mintz's studio the next day and accepted his terms.

It was on his train ride back to Hollywood that a morose Disney began to think up a new character to work on. He later claimed that he began to daydream about a recent mice infestation he had had in his office and remembered one particularly zany mouse that he used to find hanging out in his wastepaper basket. Turning to his wife who had accompanied him for the ride home, Walt began to describe the inner workings of his imagination, explaining to her that he wanted to create a cute new character called Mortimer Mouse.

Upon hearing this, Walt's wife promptly informed her husband she felt that Mortimer was too depressing of a name and suggested calling it Mickey instead. Now all Disney had to do was get the concept from his mental drawing board onto the physical drawing board. Once he was back to the studio, he recruited his most reliable artist, Ub Iwerks, for this task.

To Disney's delight and great amusement, Iwerks found an easy route to character development by taking the template used for Oswald and altering the characters bunny rabbit ears and tail to more mousy-looking appendages. And so, the story goes, Walt Disney's ever lovable Mickey Mouse was born.

Chapter Seven

The Road to Success

"I have been up against tough competition all my life. I wouldn't know how to get along without it."

—Walt Disney

In March 1928, Walt Disney was knee deep in his production of one of the most iconic cartoon characters in history, Mickey Mouse, when he received his final payment for the Oswald cartoon. Walt used this last paycheck from Mintz and company to put the final touches on a Mickey Mouse production entitled *Plane Crazy*. It was a whimsical piece starring the loveable rodent as a pilot of a plane.

But when Disney tested out the short on a live audience, the audience goers just weren't that interested. Back to the drawing board, Disney tried again, this time with a short film they called *Gallopin' Gaucho*, but this one failed to pass muster as well. Desperate for success the third time around, Walt hatched a third plotline tentatively called *Steamboat Willie* in which he had Mickey piloting a steamboat.

It was in the middle of production for this third installment that Disney took in a movie of a whole different sort and attended the debut of Warner Brother's epic *Jazz Singer*. In the silent movie era, this film was the first of its kind with audible singing as well as talking. And as soon as Walt heard the dramatic sequence in which Al Jolson opened his mouth to serenade the audience, he was hooked.

He left the theatre knowing that he had seen the beginning of the end of silent movies. He was also given the immediate inspiration to make sure Mickey's *Steamboat Willie* broke the silent film sound barrier as well. The next few days he worked overtime in the studio to have a complete musical score, sound effects, and brief dialogue for Mickey supplied by none other than Walt Disney himself. The short cartoon sequence perfectly melded sight and sound, and the musical numbers played, such as "Turkey in the Straw," set a standard that Disney productions would forever follow in future features.

It was during this sequence that another famous character, Minnie Mouse, made her debut. Minnie drops a guitar and a few pages of sheet music only to have a hungry goat devour them. Mickey and Minnie then get the bright idea to commandeer the goat's "belly full of music" and turn the animal into a makeshift record player. With Minnie spinning the animal's tail and Mickey opening its mouth wide for optimal sound, we hear a lively music score to which the characters dance in perfect choreography.

This silly kind of dance number between talking animals and inanimate objects would be repeated all manner of Disney films in the future. When you think of the singing candlestick in 1992's *Beauty in the Beast* for example, it's just one in a long number of evolving choreography routines that can all be traced back to that goat turned turntable in *Steamboat Willie*.

The smiling flowers Disney drew in art class as a child that his teachers thought were so odd were direct preludes to his success. And *Steamboat Willie*, in many ways, was Walt Disney's ultimate vindication. In particular, it was his triumph against Mintz and Laemmle for shutting him out and double-crossing him in the movie business. It showed the world at large and anyone who doubted him that his creative genius and raw talent could no longer be denied.

On November 18, 1929, *Steamboat Willie* made its main public debut, and the reception couldn't have been better. Crowds were wowed by the lively animation and combination of sound; they had never seen anything quite like it before.

Critics from the *New York Times* readily proclaimed that *Steamboat Willie* was "an ingenious piece of work with a good deal of fun. It growls, whines, squeaks and makes various other sounds that add to its mirthful quality." Disney's masterful combination of animation and sound was way ahead of the competition, and he would remain ahead of the pack for about another year.

Aiding him in this was the contract that Disney had signed with Pat Powers, a one-time bigwig of Universal Pictures and full-time opportunist. At first, Powers was just helping Disney out on a technical level by supplying a special Cinephone system to record sound for his animation. But after Disney began to face some difficulty in the distribution of his animated sound, he partnered with Powers to have his new releases distributed by his Celebrity Pictures group.

Everything was going great for Disney and Powers until sometime in 1930 when the two had a falling out. Disney apparently got into an argument with Powers over finances that resulted in Powers parting company with him and hiring Disney's lead cartoonist Ub Iwerks instead. In a move reminiscent of the betrayal Disney had experienced at the hands of Mintz, it appeared that Powers sought to steal Disney's creative enterprise right out from under his nose.

It was a tough time for Walt Disney; he couldn't find enough distributors to take on his latest productions and his coffers were running dry as a result. Disney soon found another means to finance his dreams, however, when he began to try Mickey Mouse's white gloved hand at merchandising. According to Disney, the first time Mickey was used to sell merchandise occurred spontaneously in the spring of 1930.

As Disney tells it, he and his wife were holed up in a hotel room in New York on business when a man came to their door with an interesting proposition. He wanted to give Disney $300 in exchange for letting him put the likeness of Mickey Mouse on a series of children's paper writing tablets. For Walt, who was at the time in desperate need for an influx of cash, it seemed like an easy enough request to make money.

This would be the first in a long line of licensing of Mickey Mouse for merchandise. It would be soon followed by several more money-making deals through toys, collectibles, and Mickey Mouse clubs—all with the likeness of that mouse Disney once saw poking its furry little head out of his wastepaper basket.

With the start of what would be an extremely lucrative enterprise in its own right, Walt Disney had learned a valuable lesson in the world of intellectual property rights. And even though he had had characters and artists stolen from underneath him in the past, he made sure that Mickey Mouse wasn't going anywhere anytime soon.

Chapter Eight

Impeccable Timing

"A man should never neglect his family for business."

—Walt Disney

By October 1931, the strain of work and stress over finding enough distributors for his productions were beginning to take its toll on Walt Disney. He also had to deal with increasing threats and recriminations from his previous partner Powers and even from his former top artist Ub Iwerks.

Iwerks, who had been Disney's main animator, had been growing resentful of Walt's oversight for many years. He felt that he wasn't getting the credit he deserved and that his rightful creations and artistic renderings were being greedily subsumed by Disney, who slapped his name on Iwerks' drawings and called them his own. This resentment was supposedly on full display shortly before Iwerks left in dramatic fashion. The incident sprang from an innocent enough exchange.

As the story goes, the Disney entourage was at a party when a young boy requested an autograph and drawing of Mickey Mouse from Disney. Walt Disney instead of drawing it himself allegedly turned to Iwerks and ordered him to draw Mickey so he could sign below it. For Iwerks, who long felt that he was handing off his hard work only for Walt to swoop down and take credit for it, this was about the most blatant manifestation of this perceived reality that he could have imagined.

So, for most, looking back at such things in retrospect it's not too surprising that he shouted back at Walt, "Draw it yourself!" and stormed out in a huff. Disney, however, not always the most receptive to the feelings of his colleagues seems to have been shocked by the outburst. He wasn't expecting this angry blow-up upon his request any more than he expected Iwerks to jump ship and join Powers' team. But now Disney had a real problem on his hand and had to consider the fact that Iwerks might be trying to take away another concept right out from underneath him.

And it didn't help matters much when Iwerks threatened to sue Disney for copyright infringement over the likeness of Mickey Mouse that the former lead cartoonist had helped to create. Unable to take the mounting pressure, Disney is said to have had a kind of nervous breakdown in late 1931, and taking the advice of those closest to him, he took a much-needed vacation with his wife and headed on down to the Caribbean.

The vacation seemed to have been just what the doctor had ordered, and upon his return, Disney seemed like a new man. With renewed vigor and creative energy, Disney set to work on his first in color production, an eight-minute Technicolor film called *Flowers and Trees* that saw distribution in the summer of 1932. Disney was at his theatrical best, using his imagination to bring life to normally inanimate creatures such as flowers, trees, and mushrooms.

The film was a smash hit and managed to win an Oscar at the 5th Academy Awards in 1932 under the category of "Best Short Subjects, Cartoons." This triumph laid the groundwork for Disney's next most successful production to date: 1933's *The Three Little Pigs*. It is said that Disney originally got the idea for the film when he woke up from a fitful sleep at two in the morning, and almost sleep walking to his bedroom desk, he pulled out a scrap of paper and lazily scrawled the words "The Three Little Pigs" on its surface. It is not entirely clear what Disney was dreaming about that night to inspire this new hit, but Walt always seemed to be at his best when he channeled the workings of his subconscious mind.

Disney is said to have taken a hands-on approach from the very beginning of production, often acting out all four of the main roles—the three pigs and the wolf—in front of his staff. The production team was apparently quite impressed with the dramatic characterizations Walt demonstrated as he alternately pantomimed the wolf's vicious snarl and the pigs' frightened cries. He had an exact vision of how the characters should be portrayed, and he stepped directly into each of their roles to show his artists how to portray them.

This dedication to Disney's vision seemed to pay off at the box office, with the short film grossing over $125,000 by the end of the year. Back in 1933, this figure was nothing short of groundbreaking. The film was also destined for yet another academy award.

But besides all of this official acclaim, the short left a much more lasting impression on audience goers as a powerful message of encouragement. You see, at the time of the viewing, America was in the depths of the Great Depression, and in these destitute and desperate times many Americans felt like victims of forces that were out of their control. Somehow on a subconscious level, the plight of the three little pigs struck a chord with them. In their resistance to the wolf's efforts to overtake them, they could identify their own dogged resistance to keep from being consumed by the Great Depression that was nipping at their heels. One of the songs of the short, "Who's Afraid of the Big Bad Wolf?" even became a kind of unofficial theme song of the times.

Some have even gone so far as to claim that President Franklin D. Roosevelt's famous speech in which he uttered, "There is nothing to fear but fear itself!" was inspired by this Disney film. At any rate, the impact of this simple but powerful film is not to be overestimated.

Walt Disney was in complete awe of the incredible connection he was making to his audience with his artistic expression. This film was his creative love child, and the only thing that could tear his attention away from it was his wife Lillian's announcement of the pending arrival of their own bundle of joy. Shortly after *The Three Little Pig*'s debut, she informed Disney that she was pregnant with their first child. The couple had been married for eight years and is said to have almost given up hope of conceiving naturally.

But despite the previous hardship and delay—like so many things in Walt's life—when his daughter Diane Marie Disney was born on December 19, 1933, the moment of arrival just couldn't have been better. Daughter like father, the Disneys seemed to have impeccable timing.

Chapter Nine

From Snow White to Pinocchio

"You reach a point where you don't work for money."

—Walt Disney

In early 1934, shortly after the birth of his daughter Diane, Walt Disney was adjusting to his new life as a father as well as his new reign as the king of cartoon animation. And being in the position that he was in, he found that his audience was now demanding much more from him than ten-minute short films sandwiched between features. Realizing as much, Disney sought to create his first feature-length film.

Wishing to continue the successful formula he had created for *The Three Little Pigs*, Disney once again delved into his rich well of remembered childhood fairy tales. He came up with the idea of creating his own version of Snow White, exacted from the old Brothers Grimm fairy tales. Disney handed off what amounted to a 21-page outline of the plot and characters for this modern take on the tale to his production team.

Among other suggestions compiled by his staff writers, Disney made sure to make special emphasis that he wanted to focus and expand upon the characters that would become the Seven Dwarves. Even though in the original fairy tale the dwarves remain anonymous and nameless, in Disney's version he identified all of them. He gave each of them a name as unique as their persona. He called them Doc, Grumpy, Happy, Sleepy, Bashful, Sneezy, and Dopey, and these seven colorful dwarves would end up stealing the show entirely.

But before they could make their debut, Disney had a problem: he was way over budget. In fact, with a total production cost of one and a half million, he would end up about a million dollars over budget. Disney wanted to make a masterpiece, but it was threatening to make him bankrupt in the process. At one point, with his funding rapidly running out, he even had to resort to mortgaging his home just to keep the project afloat.

It was an artistic gamble for sure, but Disney's wager proved to be right on the money, and in December 1937 when the film debuted, it was an instant success with extended showings in theatres all over the world. The film had grossed six and a half million by 1939, which was a staggering amount for the 1930s. Disney would also receive an academy award for the feature.

After the massive project of *Snow White and the Seven Dwarfs* came to completion, Disney didn't take time for a break and instead began work on his next feature-length film almost back to back. It was a piece that Disney would entitle *Pinocchio*. The story was based on an Italian children's book called the *Adventures of Pinocchio* which was first published in the 1880s.

Disney was still in the early stages of development when he received a surprise visitor at the beginning of 1940 in the form of Ub Iwerks. Just as he had randomly dropped in on Walt Disney some 20 years before, Iwerks, the prodigal artist, had returned once again. As it turns out, even though he had some moderate success away from Disney, he was not earning enough to keep his independent studio open and so sought to rekindle his partnership with Disney.

Disney, no doubt with the previous betrayal still haunting him, was hesitant and ready to lay down some pretty specific rules of engagement. He stipulated that in order for Iwerks to work for the company again he would have to agree to not take a cut of any future royalties from the licensing of merchandise. Despite this measure, Iwerks wasn't able to get a better deal anywhere else and decided to accept.

Disney then put him to work headlining his technical development department. Iwerks would stay on for the next 30 years. During that time, it is said that Walt Disney remained, for the most part, cold and detached from his former friend. Even though he was able to use Iwerks talents as an artist, he was apparently never quite able to get over his past hurt enough to engage Iwerks on a personal level.

But Iwerks wasn't the only member of Walt's team that he was distant to. In many ways, a bit of distance was a part of Disney's new business decorum. He had realized through the years, like many managers from any manner of business might, that the bottom line of his business functioned much better when he kept a safe distance from the personal lives of his associates.

Disney learned to cut out idle rumor and chit chat in exchange for an efficient movie making machine. *Pinocchio* was a direct beneficiary of this work ethic, debuting in theatres in February 1940. And right on the heels of this production was another soon-to-be hit, called *Fantasia*. This film featured a return of Mickey Mouse, this time as a kind of magical mouse wizard who gets into all sorts of enchanted mischief—all set to classical music.

Much thought and money went into both *Pinocchio* and *Fantasia*, but unfortunately for Disney, the box office returns for both were a bitter disappointment. The two films would become cult classics later on and would both be considered great masterpieces in good time. But in 1940, their dismal returns were nothing short of devastating, leading Disney studios completely into debt by 1941.

Chapter Ten

Disney During World War II

"I do not like to repeat successes, I like to go on to other things."

—Walt Disney

Immediately after the United States' entry into World War II, countless businesses, companies, and patriotic Americans dropped everything they were doing and converted their day-to-day affairs to better reflect wartime needs. And for Disney, these changes seemed to have occurred overnight. As the story goes, Walt had rolled into the studio lot one morning like he always did, only to find that the military had set up shop on his property.

Due to the fact that a vital Lockheed production plant was nearby, military officials thought it a necessity to place antiaircraft batteries and armed soldiers on studio grounds. This was done as a protective measure, just in case the Japanese, who had just attacked Hawaii, decided to bomb Hollywood as well. After this intrusion, Disney was then contacted by the government to create instructional cartoons for all branches of the United States military.

To do this Disney founded what would be called the Walt Disney Training Films Unit. He was not only thrilled to fulfill his patriotic duty with this enterprise, but he was also overjoyed to be entering into some lucrative contracts with military brass for his work. The Navy alone was willing to grant him $80,000 up front for simple animated shorts that could be pumped out almost on a daily basis.

Disney was typically able to make each short instructional video for just a few thousand dollars. This was easy money for Disney and a great way to make up for the financial drain that his last two films had taken. The only downside Disney faced was a loss of creative control and instances in which he perceived that his studio was becoming nothing short of a propaganda arm of the military. This was painfully apparent for him with the creation of such films as *Education for Death: The Making of a Nazi* and the ever infamous *Der Fuehrer's Face*.

The latter of the two featured a Donald Duck character depicting a heavily satirized version of life under Nazi rule. The movie sought to make the Nazi regime look completely ridiculous. A modern viewer probably couldn't imagine anything more ridiculous than the sight of a Nazi-uniformed Donald Duck leading a German oom-pah band consisting of Heinrich Himmler, Hideki Tojo, and Benito Mussolini, which was the case in one of the more notorious scenes from the film.

In another scene, Donald Duck is shown waking up in the morning and receiving his rationed food in the form of a piece of bread, which has the consistency of wood and which he has to use a handsaw to cut. Donald Duck is also given a single bean of coffee from which to make his morning brew. This is apparently to portray the deprivation faced by the average person under such totalitarian regimes.

An audience today might take offense at the insulting, yet light-hearted manner with which the Nazis were dealt in this cartoon. But you have to keep in mind that even by the time of the production's release in 1943, the full horrors of Nazi Germany had not yet been revealed. For that reason, this comedy focused mainly on the lunacy of living under a dictatorship in which individual freedoms and prosperity were being denied to the average German, Italian, and Japanese citizen of the Axis powers.

About a year into the war when the U.S. government came to the realization that Japan probably was not going to bomb California after all, military personnel left Disney's property, and Disney studios once again entered the civilian sphere of operations. After the end of World War II in 1945, Walt Disney felt a real need for a change in direction. And as such, he took a sharp departure from his animation of the past and began work on a series of live-action adventure films. None of these films proved as successful as his animated features, however, and Disney soon grew increasingly disillusioned with his role as a mega film producer.

Often enough, it was only his time spent during the weekends at home in the company of his daughter Diane and the girl they had since adopted—Sharon—that Disney was able to relieve his burdens and relive some of the unbridled joy and happiness of his childhood. He would put on elaborate shows for his children in his movie theatre, and he built what amounted to miniature amusement park rides on his property, complete with ridable trains and carousels. In truth, the seeds for Disneyland were planted in Walt Disney's own backyard.

Chapter Eleven

Going to Disneyland

"Disneyland is a work of love. We didn't go into Disneyland just with the idea of making money."

—Walt Disney

When Disney first broached the idea of creating his own extravagant amusement park to his brother Roy, his brother readily dismissed the notion as being an expense that they just couldn't take on. But just as the 1940s gave way to the 1950s, Walt found a means to pay for his dreams through a medium that was still in its infancy: television. Disney signed on for a contract with ABC to feature several Disney cartoons, and the move proved phenomenally successful with the ratings for his features only coming in second to the sitcom *I Love Lucy*.

With these weekly broadcasts, Disney also helped to cement himself as a persona that all Americans could be familiar with and relate to. He hosted the programs, providing brief, good-natured dialogue between cartoons, soon making the face of Walt Disney just as famous as his animation. He also drew upon his previous success with Disney kids clubs and brought a version of the Mickey Mouse Club onto the televised airwaves.

The first episode aired in 1955, the very same year that Disneyland, the world's most impressive theme park to date, opened to the public. Although located in Anaheim, California, with Disneyland Walt sought to transplant and recreate the happy days of his childhood when he lived in small-town Marceline, Missouri. This was the theme that ran through the entire park, with the main thoroughfare called Main Street USA being a complete recreation of the quaint and homey downtown Marceline Walt so treasured.

The only difference was that the replica mom and pop stores in Disneyland's downtown sold not only nickel and dime candy, but also hundreds of dollars' worth of Disney merchandise. With all of the profits that would be made on merchandising alone, Roy's fears of not having enough money to run an amusement park would appear to have been overblown. Snaking out from this little piece of small-town America, Disney presented not only recreations of the past, but also visions of the future with whole exciting new realms such as Frontierland, Fantasyland, and Tomorrowland. It was a breathtaking union, and as one critic from the *New York Times* had critiqued the enterprise at the time, Disney was said to have "combined some of the pleasant things of yesterday with fantasy and dreams of tomorrow."

But unfortunately, not everyone was buying into these "dreams of tomorrow," and turnout on the first day of Disneyland's existence did not go as well as had been hoped. Several features were just not taken into account, such as how much of a hardship the long lines of people would suffer baking out in the hot California sun. Adding to the frustration of the overheated park goers was the malfunction of several of the rides. You can only imagine how disconcerting it must have been to customers to sweat it out for an hour in sweltering heat only to find that the ride they stood in line for was shut down. Another major problem customers faced was that there didn't seem to be nearly enough garbage cans at the facility.

As much as people didn't want to litter, many found no choice but to leave their trash laying on the ground. Needless to say, a Disneyland with long lines of sweaty, angry customers whose grounds were littered in garbage was not exactly the magic kingdom that Walt Disney had envisioned. In the end, these were only technical details, however, and Walt had them quickly hammered out.

Soon enough Disneyland was running like a well-oiled machine bringing in thousands of happy customers every hour. And this was just the beginning because after having his confidence buoyed by the success of Disneyland, Walt was already envisioning his next major attraction. The Experimental Prototype Community of Tomorrow, or EPCOT, was to be Disney's next flagship to the future. But unfortunately for Walt Disney, this was a future that he would not live to see.

Conclusion

Walt Disney had few of what could be considered bad habits; he was almost always polite, he didn't utter a profane word, and he remained faithful to his wife and family until the day he died. But one vice that Disney did have was that he was a chain smoker. He had been obsessively smoking since his days of tending to injured soldiers in World War I, and he never quite gave up the habit.

And for a man of Walt Disney's era, to be a smoker usually meant smoking old-fashioned cigarettes without a protective filter, which only compounded the issue even further. As a result, in November 1966, Walt Disney was discovered to have an advanced case of lung cancer. He would pass away less than a month later on December 15, at the age of 65.

Many since have wondered what dreams Walt Disney would have been able to fulfill if he could have lived a little bit longer. But the truth of the matter is that the magic that Mr. Disney had already bestowed is probably more than enough to last us all for several lifetimes to come.

Made in the USA
Middletown, DE
25 May 2019